Presented to

_____

On the occasion of

_____

From

_____

Date

_____

Published by Barbour Publishing, Inc., P. O. Box 719, Uhrichsville, Ohio 44683
http://www.barbourbooks.com

Member of the
Evangelical Christian
Publishers Association

Printed in China.

Still the One

A CELEBRATION OF A JOURNEY SHARED

ELLYN SANNA

Happy Anniversary!

After all these years of marriage, I love you far more than I did in the beginning. Oh, life may have been more exciting back in our courtship days. My heart may have pounded more often and my stomach flip-flopped every day with nervous exhilaration. But I would never trade the deeper love we have now for those more shallow thrills.

At the end of a long work day, the sound of your voice is sweeter to me now than when we talked on the phone about our first date. The joy I find in your arms is far greater now than when you first kissed me. And your friendship is more intimate than any I could have imagined when we were younger.

Having said all that, however, I have to add: You're still the one who makes my heart pound and my stomach flip-flop.

I know this was meant for an anniversary, but there are some such beautiful thoughts in here I wish I thought I filed & said more ptn

Love in Chris!!

Rob

You are my best friend— my One

Touchstones

*I need your love as a
touchstone of my existence.*

JULIETTE DROUET TO VICTOR HUGO

Bright as Gold

A touchstone was once used to test gold; the metal left a streak on the stone that revealed the ore's purity. Over the years, my love, that is how I have come to see our marriage: as a touchstone that reveals the relative worth of the other elements of our lives. Our relationship is the standard that helps me shape my priorities. It is the solid substance of my days—and against it, God's grace is revealed in our lives, shining bright as gold.

Mysterious is the fusion of two loving spirits: each takes the best from the other, but only to give it back again enriched with love.

ROMAIN ROLLAND

*Y*our courageous gaiety has inspired me with joy. Your tender faithfulness has been a rock of security and comfort. I have felt for you all kinds of love at once. I have asked much of you and you have never failed me. You have intensified all colours, heightened all beauty, deepened all delight. I love you more than life, my beauty, my wonder.

DUFF COOPER (1890–1954), to his wife Diana

Joy is love exalted;
peace is love in repose;
long-suffering love is love enduring. . .
faith is love on the battlefield;
meekness is love in school;
and temperance is love in training.

DWIGHT L. MOODY (1837–1899)

Heaven itself descends in love;
A feeling from the Godhead caught,
To wean from self each sordid
   thought;
A ray of Him who form'd the whole;
A glory circling round the soul!

BYRON

When we reflect on the meaning of love,
we see that it is to the heart
what the summer is to the farmer's year.
It brings the harvest of all
the loveliest flowers of the soul.

BILLY GRAHAM

An Endless Reflection

I had long, intense crushes when I was young. Month after month, I would worship faithfully from afar, longing for a glance, a smile, a casual word of greeting. Each trivial exchange fed my one-sided infatuation. If I saw any reflection of God in my emotions, then He was a faraway God, a God I worshiped long-distance.

But married love gives me a very different image of God, for in marriage I am loved even as I love; in marriage, we rejoice in each other's joy. Our love is reciprocal, intimate, and ever-growing. Married love lends light to all the facets of my life—and the light that is reflected back only makes our love shine brighter still. Like a mirror that reflects a mirror, our love reaches into infinity.

Mutual love brings mutual delight.

R. H. DANA

Then I shall know fully,
even as I am fully known.

1 CORINTHIANS 13:12, NIV

A Dinner of Herbs

*Better is a dinner of herbs where love is,
than a stalled ox and hatred therewith.*

PROVERBS 15:17, KJV

True Riches

Well, yes, my love, I would like a bigger house, an old cozy one with lots of land for a garden, and woods for walks, and our own creek for the children to play in. I'd like to be able to afford to travel more, and you know I'd really like to replace our old pop-up camper that always leaks on my side. And I'd love to be able to walk into the bookstore and buy as many books as I wanted, without ever stopping to worry about the grocery money.

But when I hear your car pull in our driveway at the end of the day, I know that none of that really matters at all. It truly is enough to live each day with you, to share a home and a family and a life with the person I like best in all the world. All the little things—laughing together over our children's comments, talking over our day while we eat supper, waking up beside you every morning—make me far richer than anything money could ever buy.

She is to her husband more than a friend. . .an equal with him in the yoke. Calamities and troubles she shares alike, nothing pleases her that doth not him. She is relative in all, and he without her is but half himself.

SIR THOMAS OVERBURY (1581–1613)

*Levin asked himself again if
he really felt any regret for the freedom
his friends had been talking about.
The idea made him smile.
"Freedom? What do I need freedom for?
Happiness for me consists in loving. . . ."*

LEO TOLSTOY, "ANNA KARENINA"

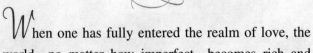

When one has fully entered the realm of love, the world—no matter how imperfect—becomes rich and beautiful, for it consists solely of opportunities for love.

SOREN KIERKEGAARD (1813–1855)

What Is a Wife?

The person who drives you crazy wanting to talk when you want to sleep, who cries for the most mysterious reasons, and yet still manages to be your best friend in all the world.

She's the only one who knows exactly how and where to scratch your back.

GERALD PARKINSON

[A wife is] magic.
Who else can mend
the television with a kick?

J. BATES

She's the person who rolls her eyes when you act like an adolescent, but loves you anyway.

What Is a Husband?

He is the household's official spider-remover and bee-killer.

The person who flirts with you on a "date" when you're dressed to the nines—and loves you just as much when you're exhausted, stringy-haired, and dressed in your sweats.

The person who can make you both happier and more exasperated than anyone else.

He is a business partner and a lover, sometimes an adversary, often a consultant, and always your biggest fan and truest friend.

Let the wife make her husband glad to come home
and let him make her sorry to see him leave.

MARTIN LUTHER (1483–1546)

Marriage is the life-long miracle,
The self-begetting wonder, daily fresh.

CHARLES KINGSELY

Duty does not have to be dull. Love can make it beautiful and fill it with life.

THOMAS MERTON

My Heart's Home

I know, my love: Sometimes after a fight I go stomping out of the house, muttering insults under my breath, daydreaming about the days when I lived my life the way I wanted, without always having to compromise with another person. But all I need to do is walk down to the corner and back, and by then I'll realize how glad, how grateful, how blessed I am to be married to you.

A life that was all mine, not shared with you, would be a colder, poorer life. It would lack all the wonder and unexpected riches you have poured into my heart. It would be bare and sterile and lonely.

Your smile is the one I want to see every morning; your voice is the one I want to hear each afternoon; and your arms are the ones I want to hold me at night for as long as we live. Our marriage is my home, the place where I am secure and comfortable and loved.

The married are those who have taken the terrible risk of intimacy and, having taken it, know life without intimacy to be impossible.

CAROLYN HEILBRUN

Love comforteth,
like sunshine after rain. . .
Love's gentle spring
doth always fresh remain.

WILLIAM SHAKESPEARE

Love's Journey

Marriage is not a state, but a movement—
a boundless adventure.

PAUL TOURNIER

The Journey

The young woman tucked a small package between two sweaters and closed the suitcase. "I'm ready," she said and handed the suitcase to her husband. She opened the car door and slid onto the passenger seat, while her husband unlocked the trunk and placed their suitcase next to a gift-wrapped box.

Headed down the highway, they passed piles of wet, matted-down leaves. Silver maple trees with bare limbs swayed in the wind. She turned on the heater and covered her lap with a fleece blanket.

"Our beautiful autumn is all gone," she said.

He nodded. "Look up there." As they climbed higher, the tops of the pine trees were sprinkled with white powder.

"The season's first snowfall," she said. "It's like a whole other world."

They traveled south across the state border, and the snow disappeared. When they finally reached the inn, they found the entrance lined with hardy orange and yellow mums.

"The grass is still green here," she commented.

Later, they strolled hand in hand through the woods. After he carved their initials in a white birch, he picked up the shavings and put them in his back pocket.

After dinner, she handed him the small package. He tore the wrapping paper and then read the title on the cassette: "Our Wedding."

"Here's your gift," he said.

She slipped the lid off the gift-wrapped box and smiled. "You made us a scrapbook."

"I tried to capture the milestones of our journey together so far," he said.

"I love you." She leaned close and kissed him.

As they snuggled, shadows danced in the candlelight. They listened to the recording of their wedding ceremony that she had given him, and then they looked through the scrapbook he had made.

Together they decorated another page in the scrapbook. She wrote "Our First Anniversary" on a piece of stationery with the inn's letterhead. He added shavings from the birch tree.

After that, every year when the last leaves fell from the trees, they traveled somewhere together. No matter their destination, their luggage always contained two gifts. They adventured as far as Barbados and as near as the local bed and breakfast. Some years they had to stay home because they were waiting for a baby, but on their anniversary they still packed two gifts in a suitcase.

And each year they snuggled as shadows danced in the candlelight. They opened the suitcase and exchanged the same two gifts: a small package and a gift-wrapped box. As they listened to the recording of their wedding ceremony, they looked through the scrapbook and traveled again along the journey of their marriage. Sometimes the journey led past bare, cold trees, through glittering snow—but always, sooner or later, they would find a place where the grass was still green and hardy mums lined their path with brilliant color.

DONNA LANGE

I have lived long enough to know that the evening glow of love has its own riches and splendour.

BENJAMIN DISRAELI

'Tis you alone that sweetens life,
and makes one wish the wings of time were clipt,
which not only seems but really flies away too fast,
much too fast, for those that love. . . .

JOHN HERVEY, TO HIS WIFE ELIZABETH

*A happy marriage is
the union of two good forgivers.*

ROBERT QUILLEN

∞

My love, I've found that the only way to travel fur-
ther on our journey is to be always willing to forgive.
Thank you for all the times you forgive me each and
every day. Thank you for making real to me the even
greater forgiveness of Christ.

∞

*A successful marriage is an edifice
that must be rebuilt every day.*

ANDRÈ MAUROIS

Stitched Together by Love

I don't like those jokes that refer to marriage as a ball and chain. I am not your captive, love, nor are you mine; our hearts are not trapped, longing for freedom.

Instead, we have given ourselves to each other freely, by choice—and each day we make that choice anew, moment by moment. It is all those moments of commitment, those tiny stitches of love we each chose to make, that tie our hearts together forever.

Chains do not hold a marriage together. It is threads, hundreds of tiny threads that sew people together through the years.

SIMONE SIGNORET

The Heart's Friend

Fair is the white star of twilight,
And the moon roving
To the sky's end;
But she is fairer, better worth loving,
She, my heart's friend.

SHOSHONE LOVE SONG

True Intimacy

I have plenty of same-gender friends, people who think the way I do, who understand exactly what I mean without any lengthy explanations. Meanwhile, my love, the way your mind works is often a mystery to me. I can explain myself until I'm blue in the face, and sometimes you never quite grasp what I'm trying to say. We're on entirely different wavelengths.

But for all that, you are my deepest and truest friend, the friend who knows and loves me unconditionally. If we thought just alike, our friendship might be less frustrating, but it would also be far less interesting.

I would hate to lose my other friends. But my friendship with you, a friendship built on commitment, on a shared life, on an intimacy that goes far deeper than simply thinking the same way, that friendship is more infinitely precious to me than any other. Through all life's changing seasons, you are my best friend, my forever friend.

How much the wife is dearer than the bride.

GEORGE LYTTLETON (1719–1773)

There is no happy life
But in a wife;
The comforts are so sweet
When they do meet:
'Tis plenty, peace, a calm
Like dropping balm. . . .

WILLIAM CAVENDISH
(1592–1676)

When a man. . .is happily, blissfully married, the scope of his reflections is necessarily limited. . . . He is no longer haunted by the face of every pretty girl he meets, for he has already met the woman most fitted in the wide world to make him happy. . . . He is no longer prone to dreams about the object of his affections, for he has her perpetually beside him.

ROBERT GRANT,
Reflections of a Married Man (1892)

*Love is mutual self-giving
that ends in self-recovery.*

FULTON J. SHEEN

My Wife

Trusty, dusky, vivid, true,
With eyes of gold and bramble-dew,
Steel true and blade-straight,
The great Artificer
Made my mate.

Teacher, tender, comrade, wife,
A fellow-farer true through life,
Heart-whole and soul-free,
The august Father
Gave to me.

ROBERT LOUIS STEVENSON
(1850–1894)

What is there in the vale of life
Half so delightful as a wife,
When friendship, love, and peace combine
To stamp the marriage-bond divine?

WILLIAM COWPER (1731–1800)

*Love is the expansion of two natures
in such a fashion that each includes the other,
each is enriched by the other.*

FELIX ADLER

Love Ever Grows

*I bless you. I kiss and caress. . .
and gaze into your deep,
sweet eyes which long ago
conquered me completely.
Love ever grows.*

**TSARITSA ALEXANDRA (1872–1918),
TO TSAR NICHOLAS II**

Worth It All

I'm glad that you and I took our marriage vows seriously, my love. If we hadn't, there were certainly times when we could have walked away from each other. Remember that time at the beginning of our marriage when we argued at least once a day, over everything from the budget to where we were going to church? Or think about that year when everything went wrong, when all our dreams seemed to be falling in shatters around us, and we took our sorrow and disappointment out on each other. Marriage wasn't fun those times; walking out on our promises would have been far easier.

But if we had, think what we would have missed: all the laughter and tenderness and joy that came after those bad spots. No, our relationship isn't always easy. But I always know that the hard times never last forever—and the love that grows even in the midst of pain is worth the effort.

I do love you. . .as the dew loves the flowers; as the birds love the sunshine; as the wavelets love the breeze; as mothers love their firstborn; as memory loves old faces; as the yearning tides love the moon; as angels love the pure in heart.

MARK TWAIN (1835–1910)

She gave me eyes, she gave me ears;
And humble cares, and delicate fears;
A heart, the fountain of sweet tears;
And love, and thought, and joy.

WILLIAM WORDSWORTH (1770–1850)

A Lifetime of Riches

I wonder why it is, my love, that people find weddings so fascinating. That one day involves so much planning and excitement. Everyone celebrates with the happy couple.

And of course, I don't begrudge the newlyweds all the attention. But really, love, don't you think people should be even more excited by the fact that you and I have now been married all this time? Shouldn't everyone celebrate the fact that our marriage grows richer and deeper day by day? A wedding takes just an hour or so, after all, but a marriage takes a lifetime.

There is no applause in marriage.
No one applauds a flowering tree.

HAROLD PHILIPS

A good husband makes a good wife. . .
AND a good wife makes a good husband.

PROVERB

If twenty years were to be erased and I were to be presented with the same choice again under the same circumstances I would act precisely as I did then. . . . I have needed her all these twenty years. I love her and I need her now. I always will.

THE DUKE OF WINDSOR, about his wife

A successful marriage demands a divorce:
a divorce from your self-love.

PAUL FROST

A successful marriage is not a gift;
it is an achievement.

ANN LANDERS

The Christian is supposed to love his neighbor, and since his wife is his nearest neighbor, she should be his deepest love.

MARTIN LUTHER (1483–1546)

Forgetting oneself is not a refinement of love.
It is a first condition of love.

LEON JOSEPH SUENENS

Love does not dominate; it cultivates.

JOHANN WOLFGANG VON GOETHE
(1749–1832)

Love is like friendship caught on fire. In the beginning a flame, very pretty, often hot and fierce but still only light and flickering. As love grows older, our hearts mature and our lives become as coals, deep-burning and unquenchable.

BRUCE LEE

Love spends all, and still hath store.

PHILIP JAMES BAILEY

The essential nature of marriage consists in a certain indivisible union of minds by which each one of the consorts is bound to keep inviolably his faith with the other.

THOMAS AQUINAS (13th century)

Between a man and his wife
nothing ought to rule but love.

WILLIAM PENN (17TH CENTURY)

Love isn't like a reservoir. You'll never drain it dry. It's much more like a natural spring. The longer and the farther it flows, the stronger and deeper and the clearer it becomes.

EDDIE CANTOR

A Reflection of God's Love

I remember, my love, what it was like to go out on dates, the excitement of first attraction, the anticipation of that first embrace—but I have no desire to go back to those days. I'd far rather have the sure knowledge of your constant love, the security of your lifelong faithfulness. These days, I don't have to agonize and obsess and dream about our relationship; instead, I can simply walk out on its bedrock, knowing it will hold my weight, for it is the solid foundation from which our lives grow.

And that is why, my love, on our anniversary and always, you're still the one who shows me an image of God's unfailing love.

Love and faithfulness always breed confidence.

FRANCIS DE SALES